About the Author

Genevieve lives in Switzerland with her husband, two daughters and very shouty sausage dog. This is her first book of poems and she is so excited about getting it published that she feels a bit sick.

Modern Day Fairy Tales

Genevieve Snell

Modern Day Fairy Tales

Vanguard Press

A CIP catalogue record for this title is
available from the British Library.

ISBN 978-1-80016-137-5

*Vanguard Press is an imprint of
Pegasus Elliot MacKenzie Publishers Ltd.
www.pegasuspublishers.com*

First Published in 2021

Vanguard Press
Sheraton House Castle Park
Cambridge England

Printed & Bound in Great Britain

Dedication

For Dan - my very own Grog Prince (and to anyone else who secretly thinks I should be dedicating this book to them. You know who you are... Joss).

Acknowledgements

Firstly I would like to thank Pegasus Publishers for giving me a chance and publishing my book! The rest of my heartfelt thanks goes to all my family and friends for their support - and just for being so utterly lovely.

Snow Orange

We're making Snow White modern and new
So we're giving our girl a tangerine hue
On our girl who has coloured her skin so peculiar
We shall bestow the name Tallulah.

On the outskirts of Staines in an end terrace house
Lived Tallulah, her dad... and her dad's new spouse.

Tallulah was a kind and gentle soul
Who hoped to embrace her step-daughter role.

But Spouse was a vain and jealous bint
And her jealousy fell on Tal's tangerine tint.

Daily she asked her mirrored wall,
"Who is the orangest of us all?"

Each day the spouse tried a different cream
Desperate to achieve that tangoed sheen.

But still the blasted mirrored wall told her
That Tallulah's skin was one orange shade bolder.

Finally, unable to take it no more
She persuaded Tal's dad to send her abroad.

She told her new man, "That girl needs a job,
Let's send her away to earn a few bob."

"I've found her a job in some place called Majorca
As a nanny for a chap with six sons and a daughta."
(As we are being all modern and new
The use of 'dwarfs' really won't do.)

Spouse secretly knew that the wages were mean
And no way could Tally afford orange cream.

Off Tally flew on a low-budget* deal
*Until you include tax, bags and a meal...

After a week Spouse just had to ask.
"Who is now oranger?" she shrieked at her glass

The mirror issued a pitying sigh
And said, "Listen, Spouse, I really can't lie..."

"While you now win on the tango front,
When it comes to class I have to be blunt..."

"Tallulah now boasts a natural tanned sheen
That makes *her* the unprecedented tanning queen."

The mirror was keen to mention quite swiftly,
"Tallulah tanned safely — she used factor fifty."

Under the orange, Spouse turned deathly pale
And let out a screeching, blood curdling wail.

Then she took a deep breath and googled 'Majorca'.
"Darling," she said, "we should visit your daughta…"

Tal's dad was thrilled to hear her say this
Usually she uttered Tal's name with a hiss.

But we know that secretly our mean orange queen
Was planning an all new tanning regime.

She smirked at the mirror as she walked out the door
Her suitcase was bulging with SPF four…

Claire with the hair

Forgive me for changing this young lady's name
You probably know her of 'Rapunzel' fame.

I've changed to be modern and in keeping with time.
(And also 'Rapunzel' is a bugger to rhyme.)

So our girl with the tresses shall now be called Claire
Which as you will note, rhymes well good with 'hair'.

Claire's streaming hair had no life-giving strength
In fact, it had nothing other than length.

Well length, plus glorious, abundant curls
Which made her the envy of all straight-haired girls.

As she passed in the street, these girls would glare
And bitterly hiss, "There goes that Claire with the hair."

Many attacks were made on Claire's barnet
The straight-haired girls being desperate to harm it.

One day a straighty spied Claire in the street
And launched an attack with a tube of... VEET!!!

The cream got to work — the hair fizzed at the root
And suddenly Claire was as bald as a coot.

As the lustrous curls broke and fell to the earth
How the lanky locked girls cackled with mirth.

Claire screamed in horror and clutched her bald bonce.
Bystanders gasped, truly asconce.

In hours the story had spread round the town,
'Claire with the Hair' has lost her curled crown.

Weeks turned to months with no sign of Claire.
Everyone thought she was mourning her hair.

Then came the arrival of a gorgeous new girl
Whose hair was utterly lacking in curl.

It hung down her back in one glossy curtain.
We've seen that face, the people were certain.

The crowd grew bigger until under its glare
The straight-haired beauty said, "Yes! I'm Claire!"

It seems after the curls were fizzed from her head
Hair straight as a rod grew back instead.

Flicking and tossing the glossy straight hair
"I hated my curls," said the new look Claire.

Which just goes to show, whatever our lot
We girls usually lust after what we ain't got.

Modern Day Cinderella

This is the story of Cinderella,
A girl who marries a very rich fella.

As our story is set in modern day
I suggest we call her Chardonnay.

And let's have a footballer instead of a prince.
For modern day purposes we'll call him Vince.

And instead of two ugly sisters to fend
Our Char has to deal with a bitchy best friend.

Char and Vince first met in a club
That they stumbled into upon leaving the pub.

In pointy high heels and a cold shoulder top
(picked up in the sale of her local Top Shop).

Char was a vision as she danced round her bag
Leading Vince to the thought, 'Could this be my WAG?'

She fell for him fast — he was handsome and funny.
(He also had shedloads of footballer money.)

There were Snowballs and Cava — it was very high end
But Char was weighed down by a bitchy best friend.

In heels that were higher (as was her skirt)
Char's bitchy best friend was a first-class flirt.

The bitchy best friend took one look at Vince
And wanted him as her own footballer prince.

She shimmied and fluttered, there was even a twerk.
She knew that her skills were proven to work.

But despite such attempts to lead him astray
Vince kept his eyes on our gorgeous Chard-nay.

The club kicked them out at half past two
But they met once again in the Kebab King queue.

Ever the gent, Vince bought Char her chips.
(She declined curry sauce for the sake of her hips.)

With his (too) skinny jeans and designery jumper
She was over the moon when Vince gave her his number.

But BBF had her sights on this man
And quickly devised a cunning plan.

Having weaved their way back to the flat that they shared,
She put into action the plan she'd prepared.

And when Char awoke from her booze induced slumber
She found she had 'lost' her footballer's number.

So while Vince was thrilled to get texts from 'Chard-nay'
It was actually her 'friend', indulged in foul play.

They flirted by text, she dropped slutty hints.
It was all too appealing for our footballing prince.

Hoping that Char would become his new squeeze
He suggested a date at their local Chinese.

Having wowed her with texts of his footballing skeels
He asked, "Could she wear those pointy high heels?"

BBF gasped in horror — she would now be exposed
For she could do high — but not pointy toed!
(The girl had a bunion the size of an onion.)

So the bitch stepped back and Char got her dream guy
And to boot waved her bitchy best friend goodbye.

Goldilocks and the Three Blokes

From the title you suspect how this story will go
But please fear not — I won't stoop that low.

Goldie won't actually 'try out' three guys
She will search online and judge their replies.

Once she has browsed she will choose her top three
And hope that the 'love site' was worth the vast fee.

Goldie's first date was tall, ripped and broad
But his fitness-based chatter left Goldie quite bored.

A girl who is on her very first date
Does not wish to talk about protein and weights.

Nor does she wish to be told that her voddy
Is a toxic poison to the human body.

So Goldie decided he just wouldn't do
And she logged back on to find date number two.

Date number two was smart, rich and clever.
(She tried to ignore his penchant for leather.)

In a high-end bar, he ordered champagne
Then swiftly began with the dropping of names.

He moved on to investments, stocks and shares,
Egotistically oblivious to Goldie's blank stares.

With a sigh Goldie brought the date to an end
Unable even to say 'let's be friends'.

So with some trepidation she went back online
Hoping her luck would be better this time.

Goldies third date was a short kind of guy
To be totally honest, not much to the eye.

They went to the pub, it was very informal.
The date was, on the whole, understatedly normal.

But this was the date that made Goldie's heart sing
For date number three was a comedy king!

For that is the key to most of our hearts
A few pints of beer and a really good laugh.

Beauty is the Beast

I've got to admit that this little story
Bears really no link to its original glory.

To be honest I found it a difficult task
To write of a man who's as ugly as arse.

So instead, I'll discuss the desire for good looks,
A thing often uglier than the beast in the book.

Let's start with our revulsion to most body hair,
The absolute need to strip ourselves bare.

Excepting our eyebrows, eyelids and heads
All other hair is regarded with dread.

So we splash out the cash, we endure the pain
All in the name of this hair free game.
(Interestingly, in places we deem growth acceptable,
Hair in abundance is considered delectable.)

Next let us look at the ugliest issue:
The abhorrence with which we view 'fatty tissue'.

Society tells us that skinny is great
Which has led to our constant battle with weight.

We drink vile concoctions (they are usually green)
Which promise to make our innards clean.

If we're honest the cleansing's not really the prize
Our goal is quite simply: toned skinny thighs.

Plus perfect pert breasts and no bingo wings
Or any other of these grim fatty sins.

Finally we come to the lotions and creams
That promise to give us the skin of our dreams.

The lengths we will go to — the prices we'll pay!
Because honestly, truly, we believe what they say.

Then there's face lifts and botox, lasers and peelings,
The vast costs of which will leave one quite reeling.

So let us recap on the beasts behind beauty
As we strive for bald skin and a flawless booty.

We pay for the hair to be ripped from our skin.
We eat cottage cheese in the name of 'thin'.

We believe that our wrinkles can ruin our life.
Some even pay to go under the knife.

Perhaps we should stop, we should simply say,
"I hate those green drinks. I am perfect this way."

Ugly Chuckling

This modern-day version does not star a duckling
It's the story of a girl nicknamed Ugly Chuckling.

Her real name's not Chuckling (her folks weren't that cruel),
She acquired the name in secondary school.

She was a round and happy tot.
She smiled when awake, she smiled in her cot.

Primary school days were her best childhood years,
Lots of laughter, very few tears.

But in secondary school, everything changed.
Some of the kids said her smile was deranged.

It seemed to the popular cool girls in school
That looking outwardly happy was deeply uncool.

Another thing that really got on their nerves
Was how happy Chuckling seemed to be with her curves.

Chuckling even dared to have her own look,
She didn't follow teenage style by the book.

It seems Chuckling's laughing, happy round face
Gained immediate entry to social disgrace.

The nail in the coffin was that Chuckling worked hard,
The cool girls agreed — from their club she was barred.

Slowly the bullying wore Chuckling down
The happy expression turned into a frown.

After school, instead of reading her books
She practiced her sullen, sulky looks.

She dutifully followed the teenage fashions,
She stopped working hard and quashed her passions.

Regardless of this, teenage girls can be cruel,
They made sure Chuckling hated secondary school.

Thankfully Chuckling was naturally bright
She sat her exams and she did all right.
(Although not as well as she could have done –
From that point of view the bitches had won.)

But *finally* school days came to an end,
Finally Chuckling got a chance to mend.

She went to uni to read Latin and Greek
And no one at all made her feel like a freak.

She found her way back to her own quirky style,
Gradually her mouth turned up in a smile.

She made friends with people who were funny and kind
Who accepted all with an open mind.

After uni she travelled and saw the world
Able at last to forget the mean girls.

Once back at home she followed her passion
And landed her perfect job in fashion.
(Turns out her original quirky flair
Was now what the cool kids wanted to wear.)

When a school reunion invitation came
She felt a familiar stab of pain.

But she lifted her chin and agreed to attend
And hoped that her smile would not still offend.

And guess what? Our girl with the round smiling face
Was hands down the coolest girl in that place.

And if Chuckling could now give you any advice
She'd say, "Be yourself and please be nice."

And whatever your dream — be it uni, travels or work,
Just be who you are — whatever your quirk.

Grumbletina

This title is weak — so I should explain
That Thumbelina was the original name.

The stories (as usual) are in no way alike
Unless you count Tina's diminutive height.

Grumbletina lived in 'First World Land',
In life she'd been dealt a lucky hand.

But true to her name, Tina could grumble,
This lady could never be thought of as humble.

As a child Tina had the most terrible time.
"That girl has a Wendy house bigger than mine."

When Tina went on her first luxury cruise
The cabin was lacking in space for her shoes.

At her twenty-first birthday one of the guests
Had the gall to wear a costlier dress.

In the duplex she bought — the best on the street
The fifth bedroom shockingly had no en suite.

When Tina got married (he did 'deals' as a job,
From this we can tell that the groom was a knob).

But he was a knob who earned rather a lot
And in Tina's eyes this made him HOT.

The wedding was on a Kardashian scale
Yet Tina complained of the pull on her veil.
(This may make her sound like a dreadful ingrate,
But such a volume of diamonds can *be* quite a weight.)

Tina settled well into married life
Albeit as a somewhat 'high maintenance' wife.

When they bought a mansion in Kensington Square,
Installing the gym proved an absolute 'mare.

When a pregnant Tina bought a Bugaboo
It was out of stock in her favourite hue.

Peace was restored as her husband knew
She could be calmed with a Jimmy Choo.

Too posh to push — she had a Caesarean,
There would be no stretching of Tina's 'down-there-ean'.

Once Hugo was born they needed more space.
"Darling," said Tina, "we need a country place."

They found the most gorgeous bijou des res
But the blasted small driveway would not fit their Tes.

The lawn at the back was perfect for croquet
But their new village shop failed to stock Moët.

Their neighbour was an eminent leading Tory
But the local pre-school was not Montessori.

The village boasted a famous hair dresser
But finding a cleaner proved a right stresser.

Located nearby was the best private school
But the school run was long — Tina's life could be cruel.

She screamed at her husband, "I want a divorce!"
I simply can't spend all this time in the Porsche."

So at five little Hugo was sent off to board
And Tina's routine could at last be restored.

Spinning, then luncheon, the nail bar and waxing.
"Really," she sighed, "my life is so taxing."

And so Tina's life continued this way,
She grumbled right up to her dying day.

And when that day came she said from her grave,
"This coffin they chose is just not my fave…"

Beauty Sleep

Remember the story about the princess who slumbered?
And without a prince's kiss her days were numbered?

Well a modern day princess — we'll call ours Charlene,
Needs more out of life than a kiss and a dream.

Charlenes need their mates, jobs (and makeup)
Not just a lingering kiss when they wake up.

So instead of waking, heart all a-flutter
These are the words our Charlene would utter.

"For goodness sake, I was trying to sleep!
So please go away you slobbering creep!"

"Twelve hours sleep keeps me looking my best
Not puckered lips from a dribbling pest."

So let's go back to Aurora's story,
The one where Prince Charming stole much of the glory.

If you take a look at the original plot
This prince was apparently rather hot.
(Have you noticed in fairy tales this happens a lot?)

However I feel that the point should be made
She'd only met him one time in the glade.

Granted they clicked — they even burst into song
Which is (let's be honest) just creepily wrong.

We can all be agreed that they fancied each other
They may even have spotted a potential new lover.

You can call this 'true love' if you really must
But personally I think we should label it 'lust'.

And don't get me wrong — lust has it's place,
To be honest it's mostly deliciously great.

But would we really want to be woken like this?
Startled awake by an unexpected kiss?

Also Aurora had slept almost to her death
So can you imagine the stench of her breath??
(Shouldn't we all be naturally disposed
To keep our ghastly morning mouths closed?)

Anyway, I seem to have strayed from the theme
Of the modern day princess we've named Charlene.

The theme being this: Charlenes need their naps.
(And quite often facials and lashings of wax.)

And much as a snog can be just the best
It can't interfere with our much needed rest.

In fact bed-time shenanigans of any sort
Really ought to be given a second thought.
(At this time of night we are tired, sometimes tipsy,
We really don't need someone getting all lipsy.)

So to bring home my point: kissing is fine
But beauty sleep is, quite frankly, divine.

The Little Barmaid

This tale is worlds apart from the story
The one starring Ariel and her fish tail glory.

I really think Ariel made a questionable choice
In losing the tail and the enchanting voice.

To give up a voice that had X-Factor merit?
In the hopes of winning a guy named Eric?

This was a girl who could breathe under water,
She was the freakin' sea king's daughter!

On top of all that she could swim like a bream,
To give all that up — for a far-fetched dream?

A dream of a prince who she'd only just met,
Really Ariel? How dumb can you get!?

So our barmaid — Persilla — worked in a pub
That served fancy gin and posh gastro grub.

But, with a tenuous link to the fishtailed girl,
Persilla's vocals were out of this world.

She worked in the pub just to pay the bills
Not for the love of serving cheese twills.
(Served upon slow-roasted pan-fried goose
With a lobster bisque and a fennel mousse.)

On nights when she wasn't at work in the pub,
Persilla did the circuit of the bars and the clubs.

But gigs such as this brought no fame (nor dough)
And her real dream was winning the X-Factor show.

Finally the show was to come ' Silla's way
In excitement she waited for 'audition day'.

When I say excitement, I mean cold fear,
In her head it was Simon's voice she could hear.

She wanted the words, 'I don't like it... I love it.'
But what if he told her just to shove it?

Her song choice was made (Cher's 'Believe')
She also had a sob story up her sleeve.

Finally Ant (or Dec) said, "It's your turn to go."
(Okay... I know that's a different show...)

She quivered with nerves but then grew strong
As she belted out her chosen song.

Around the stage her singing soared
The judges stood, the audience roared.

The show catapulted Persilla to fame.
(She ignored the suggestion of changing her name.)

From a gigging barmaid to a pop star queen
The moral of the story: follow your dream.
(But not if that dream's of a man you just met,
And don't give up things that you might just regret.)

The Grog Prince

As the title above, I hope, should describe
The prince in this story liked to imbibe.

To be honest he wasn't really a prince
Guess who he was from the following hints.

He started with cider when he was a youth,
It was Diamond White to tell the truth.

He drank it alone — he knew others would think
That this was a rather girly drink.

He (of course) had that night when he drank all the rum,
The ensuing spew-fest was really no fun.

We've all had that night, though it's not always rum
Sometimes it's the Baileys bought at Christmas by Mum.

Whatever the drink, the result's always the same
It's the one drink we won't ever touch again.

As our prince hit late teens he progressed to beer,
Well that and anything else that was near.

He dabbled in vile coloured alcho-pops,
Fake-ID at the ready as he entered the shops.

In his first year of uni he was thrilled when he found
A club that served students 'a triple a pound'.

Second year uni saw Snakebite and Black
But he found drinking this made him act like a twat.

Third year of uni he was so broke
He drank budget vodka with unbranded coke.

His twenties proved to be better years
Happily drenched in copious beers.

He'd be found in departures most of the time,
' Cos in airports a drink at any hour's fine.

Then there was 'coupled up' sofa time
When he got engaged and drank (quite) good wine.

In his early thirties he sampled real ale,
He even tried brewing it — epic fail!

Along came the kids — he turned to hard liquor
He found that it made the day go much quicker.

In his forties he hit a mid-life crisis
During this time the drink was the least of his vices.

He bought a Harley, he wore leather pants,
He was horribly deaf to his wife's pleading rants.

After an ugly incident in a pottery class
This uncomfortable phase finally passed.

However the drink was a large part of him
And he willingly sampled this newfangled gin.

He moved on to posh wine, which he'd swirl in the glass.
"Hmmm… I'm getting a hint of freshly cut grass."

Posh wine remained a constant stay in his life.
(This hobby was also enjoyed by his wife.)

Have you guessed the identity of this old soak?
Our prince is a British, middle class bloke.